This Book Belongs To:

_____

Presented By:

_____

On:

_____

This book is dedicated to our two daughters, Janelle Lyn and Renaya Grace. They edit my books. They both help in their unique ways. One will find grammatical errors and the other typographical ones. They are two very different people, but they are alike in the ways that are so important to me and make us both so proud. They care deeply about people and contribute so much to society, impacting it positively, each with extraordinary Christian Ministries. Thanks for your help! I love "My Girls."

This is a work of non-fiction. Please note the information contained within this document is for educational and entertainment purposes only. All effort has been executed to present accurate, up to date, and reliable, information. The content within this book has been derived from various sources.
All Scripture quotes are taken from the
The International Children's Bible except where noted.

Copyright © 2024 by Janice Millane Wasmer

All rights reserved. No part of this book may be reproduced or used in any manner without written permission of the copyright owner except for the use of quotations in a book review. For more information, address: wildartamerica@gmail.com

First hardback edition November 2024

Janice Millane Wasmer also authored these books in this series, "In God's Creation Animals of the Forest" and "In God's Creation Animals of the Desert"

Book design by Janice Millane Wasmer WildArtAmerica Publishing.
Special thanks and appreciation to my two editor-daughters,
Janelle L. Channell and Renaya G. Van Dusen.
Without their loving support, encouragement, and editing this book for me, this endeavor would have been much more difficult.
I would like to acknowledge Holly Youngblood Cannon for the use of some of her photography for reference photos. Thanks Holly!
Furthermore, I would like to thank my husband, Ed Wasmer, who supports me and my art in every human way possible. To him, I am most grateful.

ISBN 979-8-9907327-2-8 Hardback

www.janicemillanewasmer.com

In God's Creation
Animals of the Ocean
A Book for "Kids" of All Ages

Written and Illustrated by Janice Millane Wasmer

Amazingly, I am now on the third title in this series. I plan to make it to five altogether. It has been such a fun adventure. Creating is part of my DNA; my Dad was one of the most creative inventors I know. He did things for people out of the kindness of his heart. Nothing was ever expected in return. As the father of 11 children, he learned how to do things independently, as paying others to do fix-it projects was never in the budget. He was a plumber by trade. He put those pipes together like nobody's business. He built a swing set in our backyard, just like the ones you would find in public parks. Dad built things to last forever. We had a toboggan. He built a slide that sloped into the field behind our row of houses. When he bought us a second-hand go-cart, he had to make a track for us. He put bales of straw on each of the curves that we could crash into.

There are just too many things to tell about my Dad. The one thing that was the most prominent in his character was that he was strict but fair. He brought us up to have integrity and thoughtfulness for others. He was also proud of his name. He always told us, "Use your last name if you do something good." "But if you end up in jail..." we know how that ends. Thank you, Dad, for your wisdom and willingness to teach me how to use hand and power tools. I miss your off-colored jokes. You were the best Dad a girl could ask for.

"Therefore, there is now no condemnation for those who are in Christ Jesus, because through Christ Jesus the law of the Spirit who gives life has set you free from the law of sin and death." Romans 8:1-2

In God's Creation
Animals of the Ocean
A Book for "Kids" of All Ages

"The heavens tell the glory of God.
And the skies announce what his hands have made."
Psalm 19:1

Deep in the ocean, in God's great creation, many creatures live. From the smallest sea anemone to the great blue whale, they each have their place and their purpose. God loves them all and will forever provide them abundant food, fresh water, and crispy, clean air. He watches over them with His love and His care.

"Lord, the seas rise up. The seas raise their voice. The seas lift up their pounding waves. The sound of the water is loud. The ocean waves are powerful. But the Lord above is much greater." Psalm 93:3-4

Deep in every ocean, from the sea to the coastal waters, a vast and mysterious world awaits you. Sea anemones are anchored, and giant whales maneuver with incredible skill. The oceans cover over three-quarters of the earth's surface and are home to over 230,000 recorded animal species. There may actually be over one million of them! How would you like to explore the vastness of these fantastic creatures? Well, then, let's go on an adventure!

"So God created the large sea animals. He created every living thing that moves in the sea. The sea is filled with these living things. Each one produces more of its own kind. God also made every bird that flies. And each bird produces more of its own kind. God saw that this was good." Genesis 1:21

In God's beautiful creation, the ocean, blue and wide, the Pacific seahorse gently glides. With its curly tail and a snout so long, he dances the quiet ocean song. He hides so well in the seaweed green, a tiny animal so rarely seen. He twirls and sways with graceful ease within the gentle ocean breeze. A mystical creature with a golden hue, deep in the water, where dreams come true.

"Lord, you have made many things. With your wisdom you made them all. The earth is full of your riches. Look at the sea, so big and wide. Its creatures large and small cannot be counted."
Psalm 104:24-25

In God's glorious creation, in the ocean, deep and dark, swims the mighty predator, the great white shark. For millions of years, it ruled the sea, swimming the ocean wild and free. Pointy teeth in rows that gleam, a super swimmer with jaws supreme. Up to twenty feet long and five thousand pounds, it hunts its prey without making a sound. Its skin is tough, with a greyish hue and a white belly, a striking view. So do not fear it may swim away, preferring seals to humans any day.

In God's wonderful creation, in the tropical sea, lives a green sea turtle that is as happy as can be. "Honu" is her unique name, full of wonder and celebrated fame. With a shell that is strong and wide, she slowly takes the ocean ride. She goes to the beach to make her way, to lay her eggs where they will stay. They can grow big and super strong, three feet wide and four feet long. Honu's life is long and grand, Eighty to one hundred years in the sea and on the sand.

In God's awesome creation in the ocean, vast and deep, lives a colorful starfish that uses tube feet to creep. No fins, no gills, no tail to swish; she is a sea star and not a fish. She has no brain, but don't be fooled; those tube feet are used to keep her cooled. Her skin is tough, like "armor" strong, protecting her all day long. No blood is inside; just seawater flows throughout her body as she goes.
With eyes on her arms, she sees the light tubing along day and night.

"You made man a little lower than the angels. And you crowned him with glory and honor. You put him in charge of everything you made. You put all things under his control: all the sheep, the cattle and the wild animals, the birds in the sky, the fish in the sea, and everything that lives under water." Psalm 8:5-8

In God's creative creation in the ocean, bright and grand, lives a fish with a colorful band. They dance and dart so full of cheer; in their protective home, they have no fear. Orange, white, and black they wear among anemones; they are a symbiotic pair. A bond that no one can forsake; for friends, it is a must to make. Born as boys, there is a twist: some turn to girls they can't resist. Guarding eggs with tender care, males protect them and are always there. So next time you see their stripes so bold, remember this sweet story told. In the reef, they play their part; Clownfish are a work of art!

"Sing a new song to the Lord. Sing his praise everywhere on the earth. Praise him, you people who sail on the seas and you animals who live in them. Praise him, you people living in faraway places." Isaiah 42:10

In God's incredible creation, down in the ocean where mysteries lie, lives a creature who is quite shy. With eight solid arms and a bulbous head, it roams the sea in its watery bed. Its arms are bright, each with a mind, and it tastes and feels many treasures to find. Changing colors hiding from sight, deep in the ocean, day and night. It squeezes through the tiniest crack and never leaves a single track. Squirting ink makes a cloud, and the octopus escapes, feeling proud. Oh, the octopus is so clever and bright. It's a marvel of the ocean, a true delight.

In God's magnificent creation, penguins wear tuxedoes of black and white, which is a very charming sight. Their feathers are dense and tightly packed, keeping quite cozy front and back. They swim with grace and slick speed, diving deep for fish they need. With tiny wings, they can not fly, but they help them glide through waters that are high. On land, they waddle to and fro in a nice straight line, so often they go. Mom and Dad take turns, night and day, to guard their young, come what may. The tiny chicks grow so tall, and penguins are loved by one and all.

In God's immense creation in the deep blue sea so wide, whales swim gracefully with every stride. From the tiny dwarf whale to the mighty blue, each one has a tale it's true. Humpbacks sing a haunting song, echoing the ocean all day long—Orcas, fierce with their black and white, hunt together. What a powerful sight. Gray whales travel for miles and miles; their journey is long but full of smiles. Sperm whales dive into the ocean deep, where giant squid and lanternfish sleep. Yes, whales are wonders, both big and small, yet in the sea, they do enthrall such beautiful animals, one and all!

"Have you ever gone to where the sea begins? Or have you walked in the valleys under the sea?" Job 38:16

In God's amazing creation in the deep blue sea, where the waters swish, lives a mighty creature, the swift swordfish. With a long, sharp bill, like a sword so bright, she hunts in the ocean day and night. She can grow so big, up to fourteen feet, weigh a thousand pounds, that's quite a feat! She darts so fast, like a flash of light, and dives down deep, out of sight. With eyes that see in the darkest deep, she hunts for fish while others sleep. A true ocean adventurer, brave and bold, the swordfish's story never gets old.

"Let the sea and everything in it shout. Let the world and everyone on it sing." Psalm 98:7

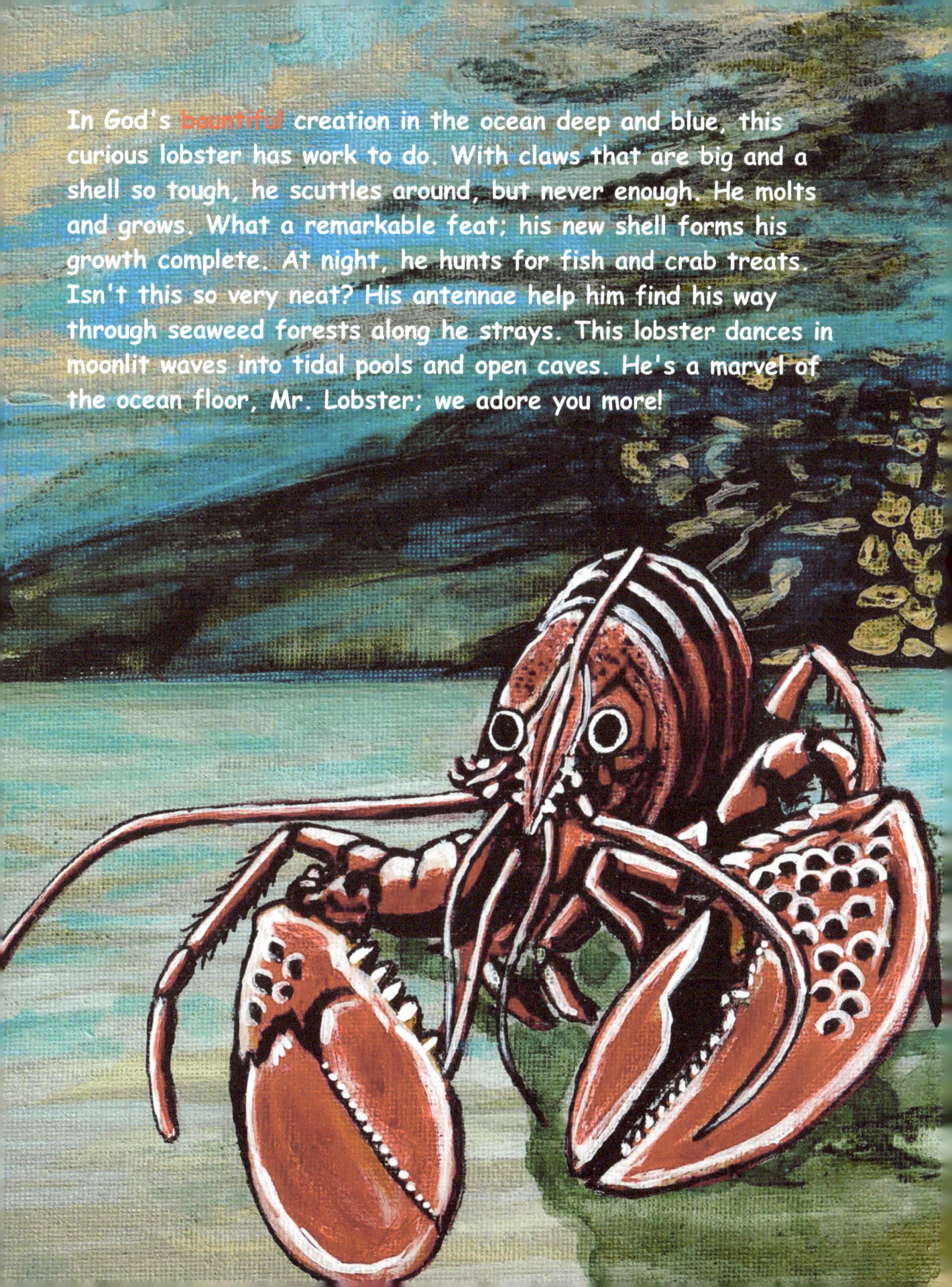

In God's bountiful creation in the ocean deep and blue, this curious lobster has work to do. With claws that are big and a shell so tough, he scuttles around, but never enough. He molts and grows. What a remarkable feat; his new shell forms his growth complete. At night, he hunts for fish and crab treats. Isn't this so very neat? His antennae help him find his way through seaweed forests along he strays. This lobster dances in moonlit waves into tidal pools and open caves. He's a marvel of the ocean floor, Mr. Lobster; we adore you more!

"But when you ask God, you must believe. Do not doubt God. Anyone who doubts is like a wave in the sea. The wind blows the wave up and down." James 1:6

In God's stunning creation in the ocean, deep and sleek, a slimy, slender eel just loves to peak and sneak. With a body long and slim she can twist and she can swim. There are electric eels that can give quite a shock in the rushing blue rivers where they love to flock. Moray eels have teeth so sharp they hide in reefs where they embark. She can slither and she can slide; this silly eel loves to glide. Some are green, some are blue, and some are spotted. This is true. Eels are fish; though odd they may seem, in the ocean, they reign supreme!

"I was there when he made the clouds above. I was there when he put the fountains in the oceans. I was there when he ordered the sea not to go beyond the borders he had set for it. I was there when he laid the earth's foundation." Proverbs 8:28-29

In God's beloved creation in the ocean, blue and bright, a pod of dolphins swim in a family so tight. Each has a smile that's oh so wide; they leap and play side by side. Dolphins chat with clicks and squeaks; with a splash and a leap, they reach their peaks. They love to jump and twist in the air, showing off with care and flair. Dolphins are as intelligent as can be, eating fish and squid with glee! They swim and splash throughout their days with gentle hearts and playful ways. Dolphins are guardians of the sea, a beautiful wonder for all to see.

In God's marvelous creation, coral reefs are a bustling town where fish and crabs swim all around. They look like plants, but don't be fooled—they're animals, and that's the rule. A shelter, food, and nursery, coral is cool. It's plain to see. It's like a party day and night, with creatures dancing in delight. But coral has a funny quirk—it's stuck in place while hard at work. So, while it builds its stony home, it dreams of places it could roam. But coral reefs need love and care; you don't find coral anywhere. So protect these wonders and let them thrive so future generations can see them alive.

In God's brilliant creation, where the ocean seagrass sways, manatees glide through bright sunlit bays. These gentle "Sea Cows," so calm and serene, are one of the ocean's largest marine. With flippers broad and bodies so round, they glide through the sea without making a sound. They munch on the seagrass, their favorite treat, with very strong lips and solid neat teeth. In the Caribbean, Gulf, and Florida coasts, manatees are animals that we love the most. Related to elephants, not cows, they graze on the grasses with wrinkled brows. So let's protect these creatures, the giants of the sea, a sight to behold so calm and free.

"Surely you are afraid of me," says the Lord. "You should shake with fear in my presence. I am the one who made the beaches to be a border for the sea. They keep the water in its place forever. The waves may pound the beach, but they can't win over it. The waves may roar, but they cannot go beyond it."   Jeremiah 5:22

In God's **excellent** creation in the ocean far and wide, pinnipeds, with flippers broad, glide, and slide. Pinnipeds are seals, sea lions, and walruses, too; each has its own ocean view. Seals are sleek with spots and stripes; in icy water, they jump and dive. Sea lions bark and clap their fins, performing tricks with happy grins. Walruses have tusks so very grand; they dig for clams in the sand. On the land, they all wobble, flop, and slide, but in the sea, they swim with great pride. From the icy Arctic to the sunny shore, pinnipeds explore and so much more. With playful hearts and flippers strong, in the ocean is where they belong.

"He is the Maker of heaven and earth, the sea, and everything in them—he remains faithful forever." Psalm 146:6

In God's majestic creation in the ocean, deep and blue, two rays are swimming just for you. Manta rays, so big and grand, flapping their wings like they're on land. These are rays, with mouths wide, filtering plankton as they glide. They leap and twirl, a sight to see, dancing in the deep blue sea. Yes, mantas are gentle giants that roam in the ocean they call home. Stingrays hide on sandy floors, and with barbed tails, they settle scores. They munch on clams and little fishes. With crushing jaws, they grant their wishes. Stingrays move like ocean waves, graceful gliders in vast sea caves. Both are rays but are different, too. One has a sting; one has a gentle grace. They dance through the water at a peaceful pace. In the ocean, they both play in their own unique and memorable way.

"'Then God said, 'Let the water under the sky be gathered together so the dry land will appear.' And it happened. God named the dry land "earth." He named the water that was gathered together "seas." God saw that this was good.'" Genesis 1:9-10

In God's powerful creation in the ocean, swift and free, a barracuda swims with glee. Its body is long and lean, with razor teeth to hunt and glean. They swim fast, like a dart, with a predatory heart. They hunt fish, both small and big, with a sudden, mighty zig. The barracuda can grow eight feet long; the ocean is where they belong. Please beware of their shiny bite, for they hunt with all their might. So, if you see one, give a cheer for the barracudas are here! A marvel of the ocean-wide, in the sea, they take great pride.

"You are the only Lord. You made the heavens, even the highest heavens. You made all the stars. You made the earth and everything that is on it. You made the seas and everything that is in them. You give life to everything." Nehemiah 9:6

In God's **astounding** creation where the fish are plenty, a pelican eats all day, her belly never empty. Her bill can hold a gallon or three, more than her belly, as you can see. Her impressive pouch is quite a sight; it holds more fish than it can bite. With a swoop and a splash, it dives so deep that she catches fish in one big sweep. With webbed feet and feathers so sleek, this pelican's life is far from bleak. So next time you see this bird so grand, remember her beak and diving plan. A funny old bird, the pelican, with a beak that holds more than its belly can!

"'When the believers heard this, they prayed to God with one purpose. They prayed, 'Lord, you are the One who made the sky, the earth, the sea, and everything in the world.'" Acts 4:24.

In God's **splendorous** creation, where water flows, lives the playful otter, as everyone knows. He has webbed feet and fur so thick he swims and dives, performing his tricks. He floats on his back, using his tummy as a table for crabs, clams, and yummies. He feasts on fish and crustaceans, too, and with his nimble paws, he cracks shells clear through. He slides down the mud, splashes, and cheers. This sweet little otter we forever hold dear.

"The deepest places on earth are his. And the highest mountains belong to him. The sea is his because he made it. He created the land with his own hands." Psalm 95:4-5

In God's blessed creation, on the sandy ocean floor, live the curious sand dollars, where the waves gently roar. They are creatures flat and round; yes, in the sand, they can be found. With a star upon their faces, they move along with gentle graces. They can be purple, green, or sometimes blue; they come in all colors and beautiful hues. But when they die, they will turn all white, a treasure found in the morning light. So the next time you walk on the ocean's shore, look for sand dollars while you explore.

In God's divine creation, Jesus' love shines bright and true in every leaf and drop of dew. From mountains high to oceans deep, His care for all creation keeps. Every star that twinkles in the night reflects His love, so pure and bright. The mountains are tall, the valleys are low, and in every stream, His mercies flow. In every creature, great and small, His boundless love embraces all. The creatures of the land and sea are all crafted with His artistry. In every bird that takes to flight, we see His love, His guiding light. From the tiniest anemone to the grandest whale, His love for them will never fail. His hand is evident in every sunrise, bright and warm, gentle rain, and the mightiest storm. Jesus' love is always near, in all creatures, far and dear. From forests and deserts to the ocean so blue, His love for all creation is true. We feel His boundless, endless grace with every breath and in every place. Yes, Jesus loves you, me, and all his creatures from the land and sea. So let us cherish all He has made in every hue and colorful shade. Jesus' love is vast and true—a gift for me, a gift for you.

"My dear children, I write this letter to you so that you will not sin. But if anyone does sin, we have Jesus Christ to help us. He is the Righteous One. He defends us before God the Father. Jesus died in our place to take away our sins. And Jesus is the way that all people can have their sins taken away, too." 1 John 2:1-2

There's still more to the story!